THE VALUES LIBRARY

# COMPETITIVENESS

Everyone enjoys being "number one."

THE VALUES LIBRARY

# COMPETITIVENESS

Karen B. Spies

THE ROSEN PUBLISHING GROUP, INC.

NEW YORK

Published in 1991 by The Rosen Publishing Group, Inc.
29 East 21st Street, New York, NY 10010.

First Edition
Copyright © 1991 by the Rosen Publishing Group, Inc.

Manufactured in Canada

Library of Congress Cataloging-in-Publication Data

Spies, Karen Bornemann.
    Competitiveness / Karen B. Spies—1st ed.
    (The Values Library)
    Includes bibliographical references and index.
    ISBN 0-8239-1229-9
    1. Competition (Psychology)  2. Teenagers—Conduct of
    life.
    I. Title. II. Series.
    BF637. C47S65  1991
    155.2. 32—dc20

                                           90-26488
                                           CIP
                                          AC

# C O N T E N T S

Competition is one way to test yourself against others.

# WHAT IS COMPETITIVENESS?

**IT IS 8 A.M. ENGLISH CLASS HAS JUST STARTED.** Alan takes careful notes. He gets *A*'s and *B*'s. He also plays the piano in the school orchestra and is the keyboard player in his own band. They play for school dances and parties and they practice every day for an hour or two. Alan told his friend Lew, "I'm happiest when I'm performing music. I love to be part of the band. We hope to cut a record. But even if we don't make it big, I'll always be able to find work. I can play keyboard for other singers."

Lew sits next to Alan. Lew, like his friend Alan, is a good student. He is also president of the computer club and treasurer of the junior class. After school he practices each day with the tennis team. Last year Lew and his partner won the state doubles championship. With his excellent grades and strong school activities record, Lew plans to go to a good college.

The physical demands of military service offer many people the chance to compete against themselves.

Susan sits in the back of the class. Some days she dozes off. That is because she is up every morning at 4 A.M. She goes to the ice rink to practice her figure skating before school. Her coach gives her lessons every evening. On weekends Susan practices and goes to skating contests. She never has time to go to parties or school sports events. She is always busy skating. Susan told Alan, "I just have to get better so I can make the Olympic team. If I don't, all my years of practice will be wasted."

All three of these young people are trying to do their best. Doing one's best is called *competitiveness.*

Competitiveness means facing challenges. It comes from the verb "compete." Two or more people compete when they seek the same goal. That goal might be a business deal. It could be a victory in a sports contest. Or the goal might be to win an election. Alan competes in music, Lew in tennis, Susan in skating.

You can probably think of many ways that you compete with others. Do you play on a sports team? Have you run for an office at school? Have you tried out for a part in a play or musical? Do you compare your grades to those of your best friend? Those are all ways we compete.

The word *compete* comes from the Latin words meaning "to seek together" or "to come together." It has been used for hundreds of years. From the beginning of human

history, people have competed. The best hunters
and warriors were rewarded. Sports and games were
used to train people for war and for survival.

Little by little, people began to organize sports festivals.
People of several tribes or areas held contests. Such
contests might decide who had the fastest horse. Foot
races would decide who could run a long distance in the
shortest time.

The Olympic Games became the most famous early
sports festival. The games began in Greece in 776 B.C.
They included many events, such as the javelin throw,
that are still part of today's Olympics.

Competition has been around for a long time. But the
word "competitiveness" has not. It has only been in use
since the 1830s. This period in history was known as the
Industrial Revolution. It was a time of many rapid
changes. New machines such as weaving and spinning
machines were invented.

Those and other inventions increased competition
between businesses. People offered more of their product for less money or claimed their product was the best
of its kind. These businesses and workers were called
"competitive."

Today the world is filled with competitiveness. Nation
competes against nation, business against business, school
against school, person against person.

Television commercials and newspaper ads urge us to compete. They say things such as, "Have the cleanest hair in town!" or "Our car is the best made," or "You can lose weight in just three weeks with our diet."

Competitiveness can be helpful. When you win, you feel great. Imagine Joe Montana without a will to win. Where would Magic Johnson be without his competitiveness and determination?

Coaches teach their players to be more competitive. The late Vince Lombardi, one of America's most famous football coaches, had a favorite saying about winning and losing. He said, "Show me a good loser, and I'll show you a loser." Lombardi was sure that everyone wanted to win as much as he did.

But competitiveness can also be harmful. Some people are happy only when they have the best of everything. They work long hours to do well in their jobs or at school. They want the best clothes or the fanciest cars. They must win in every sport they play. They may get very angry when they lose. Their anger hurts them inside. It also hurts the feelings of others.

Competitiveness causes some people to worry. They wonder, "Is my best good enough?" Sometimes they get sick to their stomachs from worry. Some people even consider killing themselves because they think they have not done their best.

You must decide how competitive you want to be. You may choose to be very competitive in sports but not in schoolwork. You may decide that you want good grades more than anything else. Perhaps your goal is to be a famous singer or musician.

This book will help you decide how to handle competitiveness. It will look at these questions:

1. Is competitiveness something that everyone feels all the time?
2. How has competitiveness affected our past? How will it affect our future?
3. Do we feel the same amount of competitiveness in all situations?
4. When is it important to be competitive?
5. What happens when someone is too competitive?
6. How can you develop and use competitiveness wisely?

You will know a lot about competitiveness after reading this book. Then you can decide how competitive you want to be.

Great leaders, like Winston Churchill, are great competitors who don't give up until their goals are met.

# 2

---

# WHAT MAKES A GREAT COMPETITOR?

**WHY DO SOME PEOPLE END UP LEADERS** in sports while others watch them and cheer? Why does one person become the president of a large company while another is happy typing reports? Is it because of hard work? Is it greater talent? How much of success is luck?

A good way to answer those questions is to look at the careers of some great competitors in sports, government, business, and music.

Jayne Torvill and Christopher Dean won many ice skating medals. Between 1981 and 1985 this British couple never lost a competition. They won several world championship titles. They earned the gold medal at the 1984 Olympics. At the World Professional Figure Skating Championship they earned perfect scores from all the judges. That had never been done before.

Torvill and Dean could not have achieved their success without many hours of practice. By working hard, they felt they would win.

---

When Winston Churchill was a young student, he was at the bottom of his class in school. He twice failed the entrance exams for one school. But Churchill went on to become prime minister of Great Britain during World War II.

Churchill succeeded because he knew what he wanted to do. He worked toward a goal. Despite his problems in school, Churchill was mentally tough. He did not listen to those who called him a failure.

There was a time when Lee Iacocca also seemed to be a failure. When he was fired as president of the Ford Motor Company, he could have been discouraged. Instead, he worked to become the chairman of the Chrysler Corporation. Chrysler was almost bankrupt. Iacocca changed it from a dying company to a very successful one. In his book *Iacocca,* he talks about the strength he got from close family life. Family support gave him confidence.

Competitors do have setbacks sometimes. That happens even to people who seem to have everything— fame, money, success. Some, like musician Billy Joel, have even thought about killing themselves. When Billy Joel found himself thinking of suicide, he wrote the song, "You're Only Human." He sold many copies of the record. He donated the money from the sales to the National Center on Youth Suicide Prevention. Billy Joel beat depression to become an award-winning musician.

Those competitors are all different. But all have something in common—a competitive personality.

A person's personality is his or her behavior—how he or she acts. A personality trait is one element of that personality. For example, shyness is a personality trait of some people. Here are a few personality traits of a competitive person:

1. *A positive self-image.* The competitive person has faith in his or her ability to do well.

2. *A drive to succeed.* A competitor wants to win. He or she has a strong desire to improve.

3. *Dedication.* A competitive person is able to stick with the work involved in meeting his or her goal.

4. *Aggressiveness.* A competitor is willing to be forceful. It does *not* mean doing something that would hurt someone. It does *not* mean breaking rules to win.

5. *Mental toughness.* Setbacks do take place in competition. A successful competitor knows that and works to overcome mistakes.

6. *Leadership.* A competitor takes charge. Others look to this person for leadership.

7. *Intelligence.* A great competitor is not afraid to seek new ideas. This person is smart enough to know when he or she doesn't have all the answers.

8. *Flexibility.* A successful competitor gives up trying to be perfect in everything.

---

9. *Humor.* A competitor learns to laugh at his or her mistakes.

10. *Risk-taking.* As a competitor sees opportunities for success, he or she takes chances. These risks are not wild gambles. They are carefully thought out.

As you read the rest of this book, keep these traits in mind. Think of successful competitors whom you know. How many of the traits do they have? Consider which traits you have and which ones you want to work on more.

## *Are Competitors Born or Made?*

Some people believe that competitors are born with great natural ability. That is what makes them competitive. Natural abilities are known as a person's *heredity.*

Other people believe that competitiveness is learned. It is learned in a person's environment. Your environment includes everyone and everything around you. Where you live and what you are taught can make you more or less competitive.

We all have a certain amount of talent. That talent, or natural ability, is different for different people. Take talent in music, for example. Some people are born with the ability to hear and sing musical notes.

We can only be as good as our natural ability allows. In other words, our heredity sets an upper limit on the

Healthy competitiveness, when combined with natural talents,
brings the greatest success.

Great competitors are often drawn to goals that seem impossible to achieve. Here, members of the Disabled Rowing Team get ready for a match.

use of our talents. Each of us must learn what our talent is and how far it will go. For example, a runner may be better at running short distances than long distances.

Having talent doesn't mean automatic success. Talent must be used and developed. Just because someone has a good voice doesn't mean that he or she will become a great singer. To do that, the person must learn how to use his or her voice and practice using it.

## What Makes a Great Competitor?

Sometimes a successful person may not seem to have great talent. Football player Steve Largent is such a person. Largent became an all-pro wide receiver and broke many pass-reception records. That was surprising because he is smaller and slower than other great receivers. He overcame his size and lack of speed by practicing extra drills. He studied game films. His practice paid off.

Other people succeed even though they have handicaps or disadvantages. Diana Golden lost a leg to bone cancer when she was twelve years old. Five years later she made it to the United States Disabled Ski Team. Golden skies as fast as 60 miles per hour, using one ski and two regular ski poles. She loves to win but says that she loves skiing itself more than winning.

Golden recalls that she was not competitive until she lost her leg. At first she worried. Would the other kids try to keep her from competing? Diana Golden learned that she could be what she wanted to be. That gave her the confidence to become a great competitor.

What, then, is the answer to the question, "Are competitors born or made?" Competitors depend on *both* heredity and environment. To be successful, a competitor must work hard to develop his or her talents.

Most children experience real competition for the first time in school.

# 3

---

# COMPETITIVENESS IS ALL AROUND US

**IS COMPETITIVENESS SOMETHING EVERYONE FEELS ALL THE TIME?**
Do people in different parts of the world feel the same amount of competitiveness as you do? In what ways has competitiveness affected our past? How might it change our future?

British scientist Charles Darwin wrote about "the survival of the fittest." This theory says that plants and animals reproduce themselves, but every generation of living things is different from the one that lived before it. The differences are known as "variations." Some variations give living things a better chance of survival than others. The plants and animals with the variations that help them survive are called the "fittest members."

The fittest members are the most competitive. They survive and reproduce themselves. The unfit ones do not. Little by little, new sorts of animals and plants develop that are better able to adapt to their environment.

---

Some people believe that Darwin's theory also applies to human beings. The weak and the sick will not survive. Only the best, or most competitive, will live. They think that the most successful people should be in charge. Those are the people with the best jobs, most money, and nicest possessions. Taxes should not be used to help the poor and weak. The poor should help themselves. If they cannot, they do not belong in the world.

Other people in history have had similar beliefs. During World War II, Adolf Hitler was the leader of Germany. He wanted to rule the entire world. Hitler believed that he was part of a perfect race of people known as Aryans. He felt strongly that anyone who was not Aryan should die. He was especially determined to kill Jews. Before the end of the war, Hitler had six million Jews murdered.

Hitler's competitiveness was not normal. He used it to harm many people. Other cultures have encouraged competitiveness in more useful ways. The Japanese, for example, are very competitive in business. After World War II their economy was weak. But they were determined to become successful. Today their nation is one of the wealthiest in the world.

The Japanese are also high achievers in school. Children believe that they owe a debt to their families. They can only repay that debt by doing their best at all times.

The focus on competitiveness in Japanese culture has enabled the country to prosper in business.

Many Asian-American pupils have this same competitive drive.

Asian-Americans are not the only group of people that are competitive, however. In fact, race or ethnic background has less to do with competitiveness that what people are taught at home and at school. Parents play a big role in how competitive children are. Some parents push their children harder to win than other parents, who feel that too much competitiveness is harmful.

In the past, boys have been urged to be more competitive than girls. Some people felt that it wasn't "ladylike" for girls to be aggressive. Maria and Megan came from families with different ideas about competitiveness.

Maria had always felt that it was fun to do her best. When she was little she was the first in her neighborhood to learn to ride a bike. At summer camp she was the first to dive off the high board. She became captain of her high school gymnastics team. She enjoyed winning, and both her parents encouraged her.

Megan started out a lot like Maria. She learned to roller skate at age four. But Megan soon got the feeling that girls shouldn't be competitive. Her dad would say things like, "How come you haven't played with your dolls lately?" And her mom thought it was too dangerous for a girl to ride horses. She wanted Megan to stay home and study.

Each person reacts to competitiveness in his or her own way. That happens partly because each one of us is special from the moment of birth. But it also happens because we learn different things about competitiveness from our families, as Maria and Megan did.

Ideas about competitiveness also come from religious beliefs. Many religions teach people to make the most of their talents. Most religions also discourage people from hurting others. The Golden Rule is taught to both Christians and Jews: "Do unto others as you would have them do unto you." Confucianism, an ancient Chinese philosophy, has a similar teaching. It states, "What you do not wish done to yourself, do not do to the other man."

Thinking about the Golden Rule might change your competitiveness. Pretend you are playing a tennis match. You don't want to lose. You want to make strong serves and play well at the net. Then you recall the Golden Rule. Should you stop making good shots and let your opponent win?

Such questions are hard to answer. They will always have mixed answers. Sometimes it is right to be competitive. Sometimes it is not. When should we choose to be competitive? What is the best way to deal with competitive feelings?

Pressure to perform during competition can bring out the best abilities of each individual.

# 4

---

# WHAT MAKES ME FEEL THIS WAY?

**DURING MATH, CHEN WORKED AT THE CHALKBOARD.** As the rest of the class watched, he made a careless mistake in addition. Everyone saw it.

"Well, the great Chen finally goofed," said the math teacher.

Chen's face turned red. He wanted to crawl into a hole where no one could see him.

Chen was a very good math student. When he made the mistake in front of the class, he felt embarrassed. Many competitive people have that feeling when they fail.

Competitive feelings often get mixed up with other feelings. Jenna experienced some of those mixed feelings. She is captain of the school debate team. The team won the city championships. Then they won at the state level. Now they are to go to the nationals. Jenna is excited. But she also wonders if she will forget what she is supposed to say.

Holding down a job means competing with others for recognition.

Feelings like Jenna's are common. But people are often ashamed to talk about them. One thing you can be sure about: everyone has those same feelings—adults, teenagers, and children. When competing, it is normal to feel doubtful, angry, brave, afraid, jealous, or excited. You may even feel more than one of those emotions at the same time.

Although everyone has feelings, they don't necessarily have the same feelings. Some of us have more of one kind of feeling than another. Some people's feelings make them act one way. The same feelings may make another person act entirely differently.

Lev and Jacob are identical twins. They look alike. But each has something different about him. When Lev faces a new situation, he is excited. He does very well in competition. He is looking forward to singing a solo in the school music competition.

Jacob, on the other hand, would never try out for choir. He is sure his voice would crack if he sang in front of others. He would rather listen to his brother compete. Lev is very competitive. Jacob is not.

Some people, like Jacob, show little competitiveness. Others, like Diana Golden the disabled ski champion, have almost more than we can believe possible. Why are some people competitive? Why do others seem not to care if they win or lose?

Each person has a different amount of competitiveness. We are born with some competitiveness, but a lot of it is learned. We learn different ways of competing from our families and friends. Remember how Megan and Maria's families showed opposite ideas about competitiveness?

Competitive feelings also change from day to day. On some days you may feel like being a "Lev." Other days you may act more like a "Jacob."

The way you act depends on the situation. Think back to Alan, Lew, and Susan in Chapter 1. Alan is competitive in music. Lew competes in tennis. He is also a successful competitor in schoolwork. Susan uses all her competitive energy in skating. You, too, may show competitiveness in one area but not in others.

How much and in what way you compete also depends on what you think of yourself. If you see yourself as a "winner," you will try harder. If you see yourself as a "loser," you may not try at all.

Wanting to be a success and needing to be proud are also feelings that are part of competitiveness. You may have a paying job already or plan to get one soon. If you do your job well, you may get a raise. Or you may get a better job.

That kind of success makes us try harder. That, in turn, brings more success. And by doing a good job you feel pride. Those are positive results of competitiveness.

Finding strength from deep inside yourself is often what makes competition so fulfilling.

For some people, being a part of a team is how they compete best. They do not enjoy individual competition as much. The 1989 United States Little League champs were that way. Their coach said that by themselves most of the team members were not very competitive. But when put together as a team they had a strong will to win. Many people like sharing the hard work and the successes *and* failures that go into teamwork.

What have we learned so far about competitive feelings? Sometimes these feelings are confusing and hard to talk about. Not everyone feels the same amount of competitiveness. Competitiveness can bring feelings of pride and success. Some people like to compete as individuals. Others are happier competing on a team.

But what about the times when we compete and do not feel successful? Sometimes we feel that way even when we win. At those times a victory doesn't seem to make us happy. Cheating or not being fair would make us feel bad. But we may feel that way even when we have won fairly.

Usually those feelings come when our reasons for competing are not the best. One poor reason to compete is to please others. Someone may get good grades just to make his or her parents happy. Those students are often afraid of what teachers will say or do if they don't do well in class. They usually don't take risks.

It is all right to want to please parents or teachers. But that should not be the main reason for doing well in school. Earning an *A* should not be as important as learning something new. Unfortunately, good grades often do seem more important. Colleges pay attention to grades. So do parents.

Many parents also encourage their kids to get into sports. They spend lots of time and money getting their kids to practices and games. They want winners. That puts pressure on their children. Emily Greenspan felt that pressure to be the best.

Greenspan was a figure skater who competed at the same time as Dorothy Hamill, the Olympic Games champion. She wanted to do as well as Dorothy, but she couldn't. She felt pressure from herself to do better. She also felt pressure from her parents and coach. Greenspan felt guilty. She knew her parents had spent lots of time and money on her skating. But she still couldn't skate as well as Dorothy Hamill. She was almost relieved when she quit competing.

A lot of people who compete feel the same as Emily. No one wants to lose. Those feelings cause people to try to win, no matter what. Being so competitive can cause problems for competitors.

Competitiveness must come from your personal loves, not from pressures that your parents or relatives place on you.

# 5

---

# WHEN COMPETITIVENESS IS HARMFUL

**COMPETITIVENESS HAS TWO EXTREMES.** Some people go out of their way to keep from competing. Others are highly competitive. Both extremes can cause problems.

## What's Wrong with Not Trying?

Those who do not want to compete are often called underachievers. Such people may have as much ability as a superstar. But they choose not to use it. They say, "I don't care" or "So what." Underachievers frustrate their parents and teachers.

Yet there are some healthy reasons for choosing not to compete. Life is a mixture of success and failure. No one can be *the best* all the time. No one has that much talent. No one could handle the pressure either.

In some cases underachievers may not really care about success. But often, deep inside, they are afraid to

compete. Their self-image is too low to handle failure. So they take the easy way out. Instead of trying, they say, "It doesn't matter to me." In doing so, they miss any chance for success.

## What's So Bad about Being the Best?

In 1981, Mary Wazeter was one of the top high school distance runners in the United States. She won state championships in cross-country and the 3,000-meter run. That fall she went to Georgetown University on a full athletic scholarship.

In 1982, Mary Wazeter jumped off a railroad bridge. She was paralyzed and will spend the rest of her life in a wheelchair.

What made this successful runner try to kill herself? Extreme competitiveness.

Wazeter wanted to win at all costs. When she couldn't, she felt worthless and tried to kill herself. Wazeter's competitive drive was not normal. Studies and research show that people like Mary Wazeter are often perfectionists.

Perfectionists try to make everything perfect. Outside appearances are very important. Perfectionists worry about what they do, what they have, what they know, and how they look. When something goes wrong—and it always will—perfectionists have problems.

Being overly competitive
can often lead to poor
sportsmanship.

---

## *Perfectionism Harms Your Mind*

It is hard for perfectionists to accept themselves or others as they are. They often say or think, "I'm not good enough." In 1984, researchers from the University of Georgia studied perfectionists. They found a pattern between perfectionism and a person's self-image. Those who tried hardest to be perfect had the lowest opinion of themselves.

Think of it in this way. Have you ever done something stupid? Probably. That does not mean *you* are stupid. What you do is not who you are.

Still, many people, like Mary Wazeter, tie their self-worth to the number of medals or trophies they win. Or the number of records they set.

Others get the idea that they will be loved only if they are perfect. They spend their lives trying to please others. They smile a lot and hope everyone will like them.

That is impossible. Some people will dislike us, no matter what we do.

We tend to believe what we say to ourselves. The little voice inside of us has many ways of lowering our self-esteem. Here are some of them.

1. *Pining over the past.* That includes thoughts such as, "This wouldn't have happened if I'd gotten started sooner" or "If only I hadn't done that."

---

2. *Focusing on the future.* You win the district volley-ball match, but you can't feel good about it because you haven't won the state match yet!

3. *Mood madness.* You set a goal for yourself, such as getting a good score on a physics test. You feel great when you get a *B*. But on the next test you get a *C*. When your family praises you, you get angry. Why should they be nice to you? You didn't get the *A* you wanted.

4. *Procrastinating.* That means putting off starting a project. If you don't start it, you can't fail. It's easier to say, "I failed because I didn't have enough time." It's tougher to admit that lack of ability or fear of failing caused the failure.

## *Perfectionism Harms Your Body*

Do you often feel angry? Do you try to do two things at once, such as eating and doing your homework? Do you always find it hard to relax?

If you answered "yes" to most of those questions, you may be a Type A person. Two doctors, Dr. Meyer Friedman and Dr. Ray H. Rosenman, have developed what is called a "type theory." It has to do with how our personality affects our body. They use the term "Type A behavior" to describe people who are very competitive.

You need to find your own balance between hard work and relaxation.

> Too much competitiveness
> can lead to feelings of
> failure and desperation.

They found that Type A people have a higher chance of having heart attacks and strokes. They also tend to have high blood pressure.

Type *A*'s certainly have some good qualities. They have a high energy level. Many are leaders. They work hard to get things done. But they risk their health by pushing themselves too hard.

You can literally make yourself sick by trying too hard to do well. Headaches, muscle cramps, and ulcers are possible health problems.

Burnout is another. Burnout strikes when a person is tired of competing. He or she no longer enjoys the sport or activity that once was fun and rewarding.

Emily Greenspan burned out competing in figure skating. She decided to lower her goals. She began to skate for fun, not competition. And using her interest in sports, she became a sports reporter.

Burnout happens when competitors begin to think more of what others want than of what they want. Other problem signs are poor sleep habits and a large weight gain or loss. Sometimes the person begins to depend on drugs or alcohol.

Competitors use drugs and alcohol for several reasons, none of them good. Some can face competition only when they are "high." Others drink or use drugs after

they have lost.  They think the drugs or alcohol will help them feel better.

But use of drugs or alcohol gives a phony good feeling. It helps the user feel self-confident.  When the drink or drug wears off, the real world becomes more painful. At first, drinking or using drugs seems to solve problems. Then the body begins to crave the substance.  It needs more and more of the drug or alcohol.

You may have considered drinking or taking drugs. You may think that if you don't try them you'll never really know the truth about them.  But consider this:  You don't need to jump from a ten-story building to know what will happen.

Many young competitors today are using special drugs that help them perform better.  Steroids are an example of this type of drug.  Some coaches encourage competitors to use such drugs, even though they are illegal.

If you are thinking about building your body with steroids, consider what happened to Ben Johnson.  This Canadian athlete held world records in sprint running. He won an Olympic gold medal.  But his records and medals were taken away when he failed a drug test.

Johnson cheated.  He thought so much about winning that he forgot about the rights of other people.  He broke the rules in his desire to be the best.

Wanting too much to win is not a problem only for athletes.  Former President Richard Nixon was also too competitive.  He used his power as president in the wrong way.  Nixon lied to cover up the fact that he had broken the law.  He was found out and resigned from office in disgrace in 1974.

Sometimes sex is used in a harmful competitive way. A young woman may try sex thinking it will make her popular.  Some young men believe that young women expect them to make advances.  By doing so, they prove to themselves that they are "real men."  They may even brag about their successes.  But such stories are usually untrue.  They are made up to impress others.  They are a harmful way of competing.

Sex is more than a physical act.  It involves every part of you, not just your body.  It involves your mind and emotions. When sex is used for the wrong reasons, it becomes ugly. Sex should never be used to buy popularity or to win love. It is not an area for competing.

Eating disorders are another problem for many competitive people, especially teenage girls. Two major eating disorders are anorexia nervosa and bulimia.

Anorexia is a very strong fear of gaining weight. Anorexics are always on severe diets. Some anorexics eat as little as one egg per day.

Bulimia includes severe food cravings. Bulimics eat until they are stuffed. This is called "binging." Then they feel guilty about eating so much. They make themselves throw up. This is called "purging." It keeps the person from gaining weight.

Eating disorders are a deadly way to try to get control of your life. Singer Karen Carpenter died from anorexia. Starving herself made her heart weak. She died from heart failure.

Bulimia causes the body to lose chemicals it needs. Teeth decay faster because they are damaged by the stomach acid during vomiting. Strong vomiting can also tear the lining in the stomach or the throat.

Many competitive people have had eating disorders. Jane Fonda became bulimic in high school. Actress Ally Sheedy was both bulimic and anorexic, as was Mary Wazeter. Those who deal with their problems, like Fonda

Eating disorders such as anorexia and bulimia are common problems for overly competitive teenage girls.

and Sheedy, now lead normal lives. Those, like Wazeter, who ignore their problems will suffer.

If you think you may have an eating disorder, get help. Tell a parent or trusted adult. Or talk to your school counselor or a member of the clergy. Remember that you are not alone.

Your drive to succeed may make you feel depressed or very sad. If you are just a little depressed, you feel "down." But if you are very depressed for a long time, you may need to see a doctor for help.

If you feel as if you want to die, remember that you can change your mind. You can talk to a parent or a trusted adult. If you need help right away, look under SUICIDE PREVENTION in your phone book. Most cities and many towns have suicide hotlines. Someone is there 24 hours a day, ready to listen.

Competitiveness can be harmful. Too little means wasted talents. Too much harms your mind and your body. How much is too much? The next chapter describes how to develop and use competitiveness wisely.

A desire to be the best brings competitors like these Miss America contestants together.

# 6

## STRATEGIES FOR SUCCESS

**EVERYONE WHO COMPETES LOSES AT ONE TIME OR ANOTHER.** In sports, someone must lose the game or match. In politics, only one person wins the election. It's okay to lose sometimes. It's all right to do an average job on a project or make a mistake once in a while.

There are lots of people who have lost but have come out ahead in the long run. Susan Anton and Betty Buckley competed in the Miss America Pageant. Neither woman won. But Anton became a famous actress. Buckley won a Tony award for her performance in the Broadway musical *Cats*. Few people recall who won the pageant.

No matter how well you do, there will always be wins and losses. The important part is how you feel about yourself after losing. How do you overcome defeats? It is easy to win. It is much harder to face defeats and stick to your goals.

When you do badly or lose, think to yourself, "What is the worst possible thing that could happen?" How likely is it that the worst will happen? Will your parents really kill you if you don't do well? What are the chances that the coach will kick you off the team if you miss a serve?

Granted, some people may be disappointed in you when you make mistakes. And you may be disappointed in yourself. You would rather not make a mistake. But it doesn't make you a bad person.

In fact, a lot of famous people became successful in spite of mistakes. Babe Ruth hit 714 home runs. But he also struck out 1,330 times. Thomas Edison's teachers said he was "too stupid to learn." He made over 2,000 mistakes on his way to inventing the light bulb. He eventually held 1,093 patents for things he had invented. Walt Disney was once fired by a newspaper editor who said he "had no good ideas." Disney and his company went on to create Mickey Mouse, Disneyland, and EPCOT center.

Babe Ruth, Thomas Edison, and Walt Disney succeeded because they didn't listen to what negative people said about them. There were many times when they were discouraged. They took their mistakes in stride and kept on trying.

Filmmakers have a useful way of dealing with mistakes. They cut (or stop) and do a retake. You can do the same. Fix your mistake. Learn from it. There's no need for guilt. Forgive yourself and move on.

## *A Four-Part Plan for Success*

Jesse Jackson said, "You may not be responsible for being down, but you are responsible for getting up." How can you get back up when you're down? Here are four ways:

1. Change your thinking.

You control your thoughts. Listen to what you say to yourself. What kind of thinking helps? What thoughts hurt?

Use positive comments. If you tell yourself, "Don't think about striking out," chances are you *will* strike out. Instead, use upbeat statements such as "Use a smooth swing" or "Keep your eyes on the ball."

Fix the little voice inside you that says, "You're not good enough." Repeat to yourself, "I am good enough." At first that may feel odd. But the more you say it, the more you will believe it.

Give up comparing yourself to others. You will feel like a failure whenever you compete and compare. You become trapped in win-lose thinking. For you to succeed, others must fail.

---

Pedro fell into this trap. He was a high school junior who was a soccer star. Pedro came home after school and wrote a note to his mother. It said, "I won't be home tonight." Then he went out and shot himself. Pedro's mother found out that he had received a letter from college that day. He had won a scholarship, but it was less than his sister's.

Pedro had worked for four years to get the scholarship. But when he compared himself to his sister, he felt he had failed. He forgot about his many achievements.

Pedro had low self-esteem. He thought the only way he could be successful was to be better than his sister. He chose to see his life as a win-lose situation.

Winning is very personal. It is *not* the same thing as taking first place. Every success and every job completed makes you a winner. Begin to change win-lose thinking to win-win. Be truly happy when others have success. Know that the only person you really compete with is yourself.

It helps to picture yourself doing well. In your mind, "run a movie" of a successful performance. Jack Nicklaus does that before each shot. He "sees" where he wants the ball to land. Then he changes the scene to "see" the ball reaching the green. The next scene he "views" shows the kind of swing he needs to reach those goals.

---

Reward yourself for success, no matter how small. Here is one way. Make a list of ten things you have done well in the past week. They can be large or small achievements. They might include finishing a book report, helping a friend on a project, or sinking a putt in a golf match. Each is a way to "win." Praise yourself for these successes.

2. Choose when you want to excel.

Decide what is really important to you. Choose the area where you want to do well. In other areas, know that you could do better—if you chose to.

Ahmed used this strategy. He is a fine swimmer. He also enjoys math. Ahmed spends his free time competing with the swim team and the math team. But he chose not to work on the yearbook with his friend Kim. Ahmed told himself, "If it were really important to me, I'd be as good in English as Kim is."

Choose what interests *you*. Erik's mom was a basketball star in high school. His dad is a fine violinist. It is natural for them to want Erik to enjoy both basketball and music. But Erik must decide what *he* is interested in.

Match *your* interests with *your* abilities. You may want to be an Air Force pilot. But you can't because you wear glasses. You must find another outlet for your interest in

---

flying. Perhaps you could design flight maps, or become a pilot for a small company.

3. Set goals.

You may have the best skills in the world at tennis or golf, writing or singing. But you won't become a success unless you set goals and work to achieve them.

Think of your progress toward goals as following a road map. Your final destination is the main goal you want to reach. Do you want to be a professional athlete? Do you want to own your own company before you are thirty?

Write down those goals. Use positive terms. Make them measurable. Then you will know when you have reached your goal. It is hard to measure a goal such as, "I want to improve my attitude." Compare that goal with this one: "I plan to make the varsity track team by my junior year."

Arrange the goals in order. For example, you've got to play Little League ball before you can be on the Pony League team.

List the skills you need to reach your goals. If you want to make the track team, you might work on sprints or weight training. Just be careful to keep your goals reasonable so you don't disappoint yourself.

4. Develop a long-range plan.

Look ahead five or ten years. Let's assume you want to make the jazz band next year. In five years, do you want to win a music scholarship? In ten years, do you want to be teaching music at a college?

Keep your goals realistic. Is the payoff worth the price? Do you really want to try out for soccer if you must train five hours a day to make the team?

When you hit setbacks, look again at your goals. Do they make sense? Which parts might need changing? If you don't make the varsity football team, chances are you won't get the football scholarship you planned on. Then you will need to set some new goals.

## *The Keys to Success*

Whenever you compete, keep three things in mind:

1. Do everything you can to practice and develop your skills.
2. Try your hardest.
3. Be a good sport.

By using these three keys to success, you will feel good about yourself. You will be proud of your accomplishments. You will become a successful competitor.

You alone must decide which of your goals are most worth competing for.

# 7

## USING COMPETITIVENESS WISELY

**ONLY YOU KNOW HOW COMPETITIVE YOU WANT TO BE.** You may feel swamped by all the things you want to do. Remember that you are not alone. Your friends and family can help when you are down. Get help when your desire to do well threatens to take control of your life.

When you find yourself saying, "I should have done this" or "If only I'd done that," it's time to lighten up. Remember the filmmakers who do a cut and retake of mistakes? Some of them have put their mistakes together in a film. They show it so everyone can enjoy the bloopers. From time to time, make your own mental blooper video. Run it through your mind and laugh.

Imagine what the world would be like if all of us were competitive all the time. When you find you're down on yourself, slow down. Cut back on some activities. Spend time doing something fun.

---

Being competitive means being responsible. Take care of yourself. Avoid drinking and using drugs. Try to eat well-balanced meals. Drive carefully.

Parents, teachers, and coaches worry a lot about helping you grow up. They forget that they can't be perfect any more than you can. The adults who know and love you may get upset when you fail. You need to know that their feelings may be about something that happened to them when they were growing up.

LaToya's mom was very upset when LaToya wasn't asked to the prom. "You'll be the only one who doesn't get to go." LaToya didn't really want to go to the prom. She couldn't understand her mom's feelings.

When she was in high school, LaToya's mom was overweight. No one had asked her to the prom, and she had felt left out. She didn't want LaToya to feel that way.

Sometimes parents and coaches are very competitive. They may say harsh things to try to get you to do better. They don't always think about how it feels to be criticized.

When you compete, you may be frightened. That's okay. You wouldn't be afraid if you didn't care about doing well. Your heart may beat faster. Perhaps you feel almost sick to your stomach. Close your eyes and take some deep breaths. Remember to use positive self-talk.

Replay a successful "mental video" as Jack Nicklaus does. Finally, remember that playing fair and doing *your* best are more important than winning. If you win because you cheated or you win but you didn't give it your best— then you didn't really win.

No one can tell you how competitive to be. You will need to make that decision in each situation of your life. Your competitive drive can be helpful or harmful. That depends on how you choose to use it. Competitiveness is not an emotion just for athletes or superstars. It is a part of each day that you live. It can make your life better or worse. It is up to you.

# Glossary: *Explaining New Words*

**achievement**  Successful meeting of a goal.

**anorexia nervosa**  An eating disorder that usually affects teenage girls who are unhappy. They become obsessed with losing weight and they refuse to eat. That leads to malnutrition and sometimes death from starvation or other physical illness.

**bankrupt**  When a business does not have enough money to pay its employees and/or its creditors.

**binging**  Eating a great deal.

**burnout**  An emotional condition that arises when a person has worked too hard and for too long without getting enough satisfaction from the work.

**depression**  Deep sadness. Being inactive, wanting to sleep all the time, having difficulty in thinking and concentrating, lacking appetite, and having suicidal feelings are all common characteristics of depression.

**discipline**  The will to make oneself do the work needed to accomplish something.

**environment**  The objects and conditions that surround each living thing. A city ghetto, for example, is an environment in which some poor people live.

**heredity**  The natural abilities and characteristics that living things have at birth.

**instinct**  A natural impulse to act a certain way. It is more a feeling than a conscious thought. When a baby is born, its instinct tells it to cry when it needs something.

**perfectionist**  A  person who must do everything exactly right.

**personality traits**  The elements of your behavior, for example, whether you are shy or outgoing  or have a sense of humor. You are born with some personality traits; others you take on as you grow up.

---

**philosophy** The general beliefs, concepts, and attitudes of a person or a group of people. For example, a political party is based on a philosophy of how to run a government.

**procrastination** Putting off until later what you should do now.

**purging** Making yourself vomit, usually after you have eaten a great deal ("binged").

**self-esteem** A person's feeling of self-worth; how much one values and respects oneself.

**steroids** Illegal drugs that make an athlete perform better.

**suicide** The act of taking your own life.

**underachiever** A person who does not fully use all of his or her talents and abilities.

# For Further Reading

Adderholdt-Elliott, Miriam. *Perfectionism: What's Bad About Being Too good?* Minneapolis, MN: Free Spirit, 1987. This book helps you find out if you're a perfectionist. It discusses what to do about it.

Allen, Anne. *Sports for the Handicapped.* New York: Walker and Company, 1981. The competitions described are in skiing, wheelchair basketball, swimming, track and field, football, and horseback riding.

Hyde, Margaret O. *Is This Kid "Crazy"? Understanding Unusual Behavior.* Philadelphia: The Westminster Press, 1983. This book includes a section on eating disorders.

Kaufman, Gershen and Raphael Lev. *Stick Up for Yourself.* Minneapolis, MN: Free Spirit, 1990. The authors give real-life examples of ways to use positive self-talk.

McCutcheon, Randall. *Get Off My Brain: A Survival Guide for Lazy Students.* Minneapolis, MN: Free Spirit, 1985. Using humor, the author shows ways to improve skills in researching, taking tests, and writing papers.

Woods, Karl M. *The Sports Success Book: The Athlete's Guide to Sports Achievement.* Austin, TX: Copperfield Press, 1985. This book includes self-tests to decide if you have a competitive personality. It describes ways to increase your competitiveness.

# INDEX

## A

Aggressiveness, 15
Alcohol use, 40-42
Anorexia nervosa, 43, 45
Anton, Susan, 47

## B

Behavior types, 38, 40
Buckley, Betty, 47
Bulimia, 43
Burnout, 40

## C

Carpenter, Karen, 43
Churchill, Winston, 14
Competitive personality, 15-16
Competitiveness
  boys vs. girls, 24
  dangers of, 10, 35-45
  definition of, 8
  feelings and, 27-33
  history of, 8-9

## D

Darwin, Charles, 21-22
Dean, Christopher, 13
Dedication, 15
Depression, 45
Disney, Walt, 48
Drug use, 40-42

## E

Eating disorders, 43
Edison, Thomas, 48
Environment, 19, 21

## F

Fittest members, 21
Flexibility, 15

Fonda, Jane, 43
Friedman, Meyer, 38

## G

Goal setting, 52
Golden, Diana, 19, 28
Golden Rule, 25
Greenspan, Emily, 33, 40

## H

Hamill, Dorothy, 33
Health problems, 40
Heredity, 16, 19
Hitler, Adolph, 22
Humor, 16

## I

Iacocca, Lee, 14
Industrial Revolution, 9
Intelligence, 15

## J

Jackson, Jesse, 49
Japanese, 22
Jews, 22
Joel, Billy, 14
Johnson, Ben, 42
Johnson, Magic, 10

## L

Largent, Steve, 19
Leadership, 15
Little League championship, 32
Lombardi, Vince, 10
Long-range planning, 53

## M

Mental toughness, 15
Montana, Joe, 10

## About the Author

Karen Bornemann Spies was an elementary school teacher and vice-principal before embarking on a second career in publishing. She has written school curriculum as well as several books for young people. Currently, Ms. Spies teaches writing at the community college level and offers workshops for young writers. She lives with her husband and two children in Colorado, where she teaches skiing on the weekends.

## Photo Credits and Acknowledgments

*Cover Photo: Mary Lauzon*
*Photos on pages 2,36,41: Charles Waldren; pages 7,17,26,39,44,54: Mary Lauzon; page 9: Stephanie FitzGerald; pages 12–18, 23,46: Wide World Photo; pages 20,28,34: Stuart Rabinowitz; pages 30 and 31: Barbara Kirk.*

**Design and Production:** Blackbirch Graphics, Inc.